WELCOME TO

THE SMASHING
TENNIS QUIZ BOOK

Lunar Press is an independent publishing
company that cares greatly about the
accuracy of its content.

If you notice any inaccuracies or have
anything that you would like to discuss,
then please email us at
<u>lunarpresspublishers@gmail.com.</u>

Enjoy!

IF YOU ENJOY THIS BOOK, CHECK OUT...

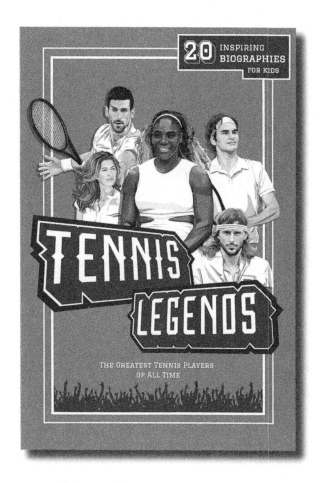

Looking for your next read?

'Tennis Legends: 20 Inspiring Biographies For Kids' is the **perfect gift** to encourage perseverance and hard-work, reduce screen-time, and to **teach your child about the great sport of tennis!**

'In one of the most emotional moments in tennis history, Federer left the sport with an unforgettable legacy and a fulfilled attitude: "This is exactly what I hoped for: To be content at the end of my career".'

Tennis Legends

CONTENTS

Guess the Player   7

Records   13

Grand Slams   18

Terminology   24

Oldest & Youngest   26

Tennis Through the Decades   28

Controversies & Scandals   40

Guess the Tournament   42

Rules   45

Doubles   47

Tennis by Country   50

Olympics   52

Match the Name   55

Match the Nationality   57

ATP by Numbers   59

WTA by Numbers   62

ANSWERS

Guess the Player   66

Records   67

Grand Slams   68

Terminology   70

Oldest & Youngest   71

Tennis Through the Decades   72

Controversies & Scandals   76

Guess the Tournament   77

Rules   78

Doubles   79

Tennis by Country   80

Olympics   81

Match the Name   82

Match the Nationality   83

ATP by Numbers   85

WTA by Numbers   88

GUESS THE PLAYER

1. This flamboyant Frenchman was born in 1986. He reached a career-high ranking of six in 2016, but he is perhaps best known for his style, flair, and flashy shot-making.

2. This Italian woman is 37 years old and achieved a career-high ranking of five in 2013. Despite having one of the slowest serves on tour, she reached the final of the French Open in 2012 and is a five-time doubles Grand Slam champion, boasting at least one doubles win at each major.

3. This robot-like former Russian pro reached a career-high ranking of three in 2006. He won 21 career titles, made four Grand Slam semi-finals, and got his best result in 2009 when he won the ATP Finals, beating Juan Martín del Potro in the final.

4. This former American pro is a three-time Grand Slam champion and was the year-end world number one four times from 1998 to 2005. She won 55 career titles before retiring in 2010.

5. This 6-foot-5 Italian powerhouse boasts one of the most powerful forehands on tour. He has made the quarter-finals or better at every Grand Slam, with his best performance coming in 2021, when he lost to Djokovic in the Wimbledon final.

6. This 1998-born American player burst onto the scene in 2020 when she won the Australian Open and made the finals of the French Open. She has struggled for form since then, briefly dropping out of the top 200 in 2022, but she is back in the world's top 50 and seems to be regaining her old form.

7. This Frenchman, born in 1984, has one of the most laid-back styles we have ever seen. He won 14 career titles, reached a career-high ranking of six in 2009, and beat Federer the first two times they met.

8. This Serbian woman is one of four players in history to reach world number one without ever winning a Grand Slam.

9. This 5-foot-9 British player reached a career-high ranking of 21 in 2023. He received a one-year drug ban in 2017 but bounced back well to play the best tennis of his career, even beating Djokovic in straight sets at the Monte Carlo Masters in 2021.

10. This Russian player won the US Open in 2004 and the French Open in 2009. She won 18 career titles and spent 24 weeks as world number two before retiring in 2021.

11. This bombastic player became the only Latvian player in history to reach the top 10 when he became world number 10 in June 2014 after his career-best Grand Slam run at the French Open, where he reached the semi-final.

12. This player became the first Canadian to win a major in 2019 when she beat Serena Williams in the US Open final.

13. This Austrian player turned pro in 1999. He reached the semi-finals of the French Open in 2010 and achieved his highest career ranking one year later of eight in the world.

14. This German player turned pro in 2006 and achieved a career-high ranking of 12. She won four career titles, but her standout tournament was in 2013 when she reached the final of Wimbledon.

15. This Spanish grinder is one of the best clay-courters of recent times. He won the French Open in 1998 and reached the top of the world rankings one year later.

16. This American star won the US Open in 2017 and reached a career-high ranking of three one year later. She has struggled for consistency since then, but she won her eighth career title in April 2024.

17. This Argentinian player shocked the world in 2004 when he came back from two sets to love down against Guillermo Coria in the final of the French Open to win his only Grand Slam.

18. This American current star reached the final of the Australian Open in 2022, the same year that she achieved her career-high ranking of seven in the world. Despite announcing her retirement at the end of 2024, she went on one of the best runs of her career to start the year, picking up titles at both the Miami and Charleston Opens.

19. This Lithuanian player reached a career-high ranking of 50 in 2016, making him the first and only Lithuanian to enter the ATP top 50 in history.

20. This Czech serve and volleyer reached a career-high ranking of two in 1997. Her greatest performance was at Wimbledon in 1998, where she won her only Grand Slam.

21. This flashy Jamaican-German player is best known for beating Nadal at Halle in 2014 and then Wimbledon in 2015.

22. This player became the first Brazilian woman in history to enter the WTA top 10 in June 2023, when she reached her career-high ranking of 10. She has won three career titles so far and reached the semi-finals of the French Open in 2023.

23. This American player recently reached a career-high ranking of 15 on the ATP Tour. However, he is perhaps best known for having one of the greatest sporting families in history. His father was a former world number two tennis player, his mother a former top 30 tennis player, and his sister is first in the women's golf world rankings.

24. This former Russian pro made two Grand Slam finals in 2004 at the French Open and US Open, made seven other major semi-finals, and won the singles Olympic gold in 2008. She reached a career-high ranking of three in the world in 2009 and retired one year later in 2010.

25. This up-and-coming French tennis player was born in 2004 and has already won two ATP titles. He reached a career-high ranking of 20 in July 2024 and reached the fourth round of Wimbledon in the same year.

26. This 2002-born Canadian star reached the final of the 2021 US Open before losing to surprise winner Emma Raducanu.

27. This 1988-born French lefty has one of the most unorthodox games on tour. He has played the best tennis of his life as he has gone well into his thirties and achieved a career-high ranking of 17 in January 2024.

28.   This Spanish player reached a career-high ranking of two in April 2022 but has since struggled for form. She has been a mainstay in the media over the last few years due to her on-off relationship with Stefanos Tsitsipas.

29.   This player is the number one ranked Indian men's player on tour as of September 2024. He was born in August 1997 and reached a career-high ranking of 68 in July 2024.

30.   This British tennis player was born in July 1996 and reached a career-high ranking of 75 in July 2024. She has twice reached the third round of Wimbledon and made the mixed doubles final with Joe Salisbury at Wimbledon in 2021.

RECORDS

1. As of September 2024, which player holds the men's record for the most Grand Slam appearances alongside Roger Federer with 81?
a. Stan Wawrinka   b. Richard Gasquet
c. Fabrice Santoro   d. Feliciano López

2. Martina Navratilova went on the biggest winning streak in tennis history from 1984 to 1986. How many matches did she win in a row?
a. 54   b. 65   c. 74   d. 86

3. Which player holds the ATP Tour tournament wins record, winning a staggering 109 times?
a. Roger Federer   b. Novak Djokovic
c. John McEnroe   d. Jimmy Connors

4. Which player holds the record for the most Grand Slam finals reached on the WTA Tour with 34?
a. Martina Navratilova   b. Chris Evert
c. Serena Williams   d. Steffi Graf

5. Novak Djokovic holds the men's record for the most ATP Finals titles. How many times has he won the prestigious event as of September 2024?
a. 5   b. 6   c. 7   d. 8

6. Which of the following women holds the record for the most Year End Championship titles with eight?
a. Martina Navratilova   b. Serena Williams
c. Monica Seles   d. Steffi Graf

7. Which big-server is recorded to have hit the fastest serve in history in 2012 with a speed of 163 mph (263 km/h)?
a. John Isner   b. Andy Roddick
c. Milos Raonic   d. Sam Groth

8. Serena Williams has completely dominated this WTA 1000 event, winning it an astonishing eight times, three more than anyone has won at any other 1000 event. Which tournament is this?
a. Rome   b. Indian Wells   c. Beijing   d. Miami

9. Other than Djokovic, who is the only other men's player to have won all four majors, the Olympics and the Year End Finals?
a. Rafa Nadal   b. Ivan Lendl
c. Andre Agassi   d. Stefan Edberg

10. Margaret Court holds the record for the most women's Grand Slam titles, but how many has she won?
a. 21   b. 22   c. 23   d. 24

11. Which player is the only man in history to have won the Calendar Grand Slam, meaning all four majors in a calendar year?

12. Margaret Court holds the record for the most tournaments won in a single season, doing so in 1970. How many tournaments did she win?
a. 17   b. 21   c. 25   d. 29

13. Which player broke the men's record for the most aces hit in a three-set match, hitting an astonishing 47 at Queens in 2024?

14. Two women's players have won over 1000 singles matches in their careers. Which two of the following are they?
a. Chris Evert   b. Venus Williams
c. Steffi Graf   d. Serena Williams
e. Martina Navratilova

15. Which player holds the record for the most Grand Slams won by an American man?

16. America has dominated women's Grand Slams since the open era, winning a combined 88 majors. Which two countries are in second and third place with a combined 25 and 24 wins?
a. Belgium   b. Czech Republic   c. Russia
d. Germany   e. Australia

17. Novak Djokovic is the only Serbian male player to have won a Grand Slam in the open era. Where has he single-handedly put Serbia in the combined winners Grand Slam list in the open era as of September 2024?
a. 2nd   b. 3rd   c. 4th   d. 5th

18. Who is the only player in history to have won the Calendar Golden Slam, meaning she won all four majors and the Olympics in the same year?
a. Steffi Graf   b. Serena Williams
c. Martina Navratilova   d. Justine Henin

19. What is the name of the 5 ft 6 in (1.68 m) Belgian tennis player who is the shortest man ever to be ranked inside the top 30 in the world?

20. Who is the tallest woman ever to have won Wimbledon, standing at 6 ft 2 ½ in (1.89 m)?
a. Venus Williams   b. Lindsay Davenport
c. Maria Sharapova   d. Elena Rybakina

21. Two men hold the record as being the only players under six foot to have won Wimbledon over the last 30 years. Which two players are they?

22. Francesca Schiavone and Svetlana Kuznetsova played the longest women's Grand Slam match in history in 2011, with the Italian winning 16-14 in the third set. Just how long was the match?
a. 4 hours 18 minutes   b. 4 hours 44 minutes
c. 5 hours 29 minutes   d. 6 hours 2 minutes

23. Which two players played perhaps the most epic match in tennis history in the first round of Wimbledon in 2010, in a match that lasted 11 hours and 5 minutes?

24. What was the score in the fifth set of that crazy match?
a. 66-64 b. 68-66 c. 70-68 d. 72-70

25. Steffi Graf has spent the longest time ranked number one in the world on the women's your, but how many weeks did she hold that top spot?
a. 308 b. 332 c. 359 d. 377

GRAND SLAMS

1. In which year did Björn Borg first win Wimbledon?
a. 1973   b. 1974   c. 1975   d. 1976

2. How many ranking points do men and women get for winning a Grand Slam?
a. 1500   b. 2000   c. 2500   d. 3000

3. Which Spaniard became the second woman from her country to win the French Open in 2016?

4. Which American became the first man to win the US Open in the open era, doing so in 1968?
a. Arthur Ashe   b. Stan Smith
c. Jimmy Connors   d. Tony Trabert

5. Which woman won three consecutive Australian Opens from 1997-1999?

6. Between 2010-2019, how many Grand Slams were won by men who were not Federer, Djokovic or Nadal?
a. 5   b. 6   c. 7   d. 8

7. Can you name all the men's players who were not the Big Three who won majors in this decade?

8. In which year did Caroline Wozniacki win her only Grand Slam?
a. 2017 b. 2018 c. 2019 d. 2020

9. How many majors did Ashleigh Barty win before announcing her shock retirement in 2022?
a. 1 b. 2 c. 3 d. 4

10. In which year did Fred Perry win his third and final Wimbledon title?
a. 1936 b. 1937 c. 1938 d. 1939

11. Li Na won two Grand Slams in her career in 2011 and 2014. Which two were they?

12. How many times has the 'King of Clay' Rafael Nadal won the French Open?
a. 11 b. 12 c. 13 d. 14

13. In which year did Venus Williams win her seventh and last major?
a. 2008 b. 2010 c. 2013 d. 2015

14. Which Spanish player won his only Grand Slam at the French Open in 2002, beating Juan Carlos Ferrero in four sets in the final?

15. Wimbledon had the largest prize money up for grabs of all majors in 2024. How much did the winners receive?
a. £2.1 million ($2.8 million)
b. £2.4 million ($3.2 million)
c. £2.7 million ($3.6 million)

16. All four majors started in different years. Can you place them in order of first to last?

17. Other than Ash Barty, who is the only other Australian woman to have won a major in the 21st century?

18. Four men outside of Europe and North America have won majors in the 21st century. How many can you name?

19. From the year 2000-2023, which continent won more women's majors: Europe or North America?

20. What is the name of the Ecuadorian men's tennis player who won the French Open in 1990?

21. The title of best-ever women's teenager is highly competitive, but most would argue it belongs to Monica Seles. How many Grand Slams did she win while still a teen?
a. 6   b. 7   c. 8   d. 9

22. In which year did Roger Federer win his first major?
a. 2003   b. 2004   c. 2005   d. 2006

23. How many majors did Virginia Wade win over her career?
a. 1   b. 2   c. 3   d. 4

24. Who did Djokovic beat in the final of the 2008 Australian Open to win his first major?
a. Roger Federer   b. Jo-Wilfried Tsonga
c. Marat Safin   d. David Nalbandian

25. What is the name of the Czech women's player who won all four of her Grand Slams in the 1980s, winning every major apart from Wimbledon?

26. In which year did Andy Murray win his first Grand Slam?
a. 2011   b. 2012   c. 2013   d. 2014

27. Which major did Murray win in this year?

28. What is the name of the two Italian women to have won a major in the 21st century?

29. How old was Maria Sharapova when she won her first major at Wimbledon in 2004?
a. 15   b. 16   c. 17   d. 18

30. Who was the last Swedish men's player to win a major?

31. Which major did Serbian player Ana Ivanovic win in 2008?

32. Which Australian player won back-to-back men's US Open titles in 1997 and 1998?

33. Belgian players dominated women's tennis at the start of the 21st century. How many combined majors have they won since the year 2000?
a. 11   b. 14   c. 16   d. 19

34. In which year did the big-serving Croat Goran Ivanišević win Wimbledon?
a. 1998   b. 1999   c. 2000   d. 2001

35. How many majors has Victoria Azarenka won so far in her career?
a. 0   b. 1   c. 2   d. 3

36. How many major finals did Ivan Lendl lose in before finally getting his first title?
a. 3   b. 4   c. 5   d. 6

37. Which Latvian player won her only major to date at the French Open in 2017?

38. How many majors did Australian legend John Newcombe win over his career?
a. 4   b. 5   c. 6   d. 7

39. In which year did Amélie Mauresmo win her only two Grand Slams?
a. 2000   b. 2002   c. 2004   d. 2006

40. In which year did Rafa Nadal win his first title at the French Open?
a. 2004   b. 2005   c. 2006   d. 2007

41. How many majors did Evonne Goolagong Cawley win over her distinguished career?
a. 3   b. 5   c. 7   d. 9

42. Which Romanian men's player and former world number one won two Grand Slams in 1972 and 1973?

43. How many Wimbledon singles titles did tennis icon Billie Jean King win?
a. 6   b. 8   c. 10   d. 11

44. How many majors did Roger Federer win from 2010 onwards?
a. 5   b. 6   c. 7   d. 8

45. Jennifer Capriati won three career majors over two consecutive years. Which years were they?
a. 1995 & 1996   b. 1997 & 1998
c. 1999 & 2000   d. 2001 & 2002

TERMINOLOGY

1. What scoreline does it mean if you 'double-bagel' someone in a match?

2. Which of the following is a word used when a player's shot hits the frame of the racket and goes where it is not supposed to?
a. Edge   b. Corner   c. Slice   d. Shank

3. Which two of the following words are used to describe the trickshot where a player hits the ball between their legs after being lobbed?
a. Tweener   b. Heel shot   c. Snake-eye
d. Hotdog   e. Sizzler

4. What is a topspin serve usually known as?
a. Punch serve   b. Slider
c. Bouncer   d. Kick serve

5. What is the computer system called which players can use if they wish to challenge a shot?

6. What is the shot called when a player is at the net and hits the ball immediately after it has bounced?
a. Volley   b. Semi volley
c. Mixed volley   d. Half volley

7. What is it called if a player wins a point against the other player's serve in a tiebreak?
a. Mini break   b. Small break
c. Half break   d. Double break

8. Which two of the following are names for a 10-point tiebreak in tennis, which has recently been introduced to the fifth set of all Grand Slams?
a. Mega tiebreak   b. Long tiebreak
c. Super tiebreak   d. Ending tiebreak
e. Match tiebreak

9. What would a serve in tennis be described as if you served towards the centre service line from the deuce side?
a. T serve   b. Body serve
c. Wide serve   d. Corner serve

10. What is a shot in tennis called if it has no spin on it at all?
a. Plain   b. Basic   c. Flat   d. Cold

OLDEST & YOUNGEST

1. In 1989, this man became the youngest men's Grand Slam champion in the open era when he won the French Open at 17 years, 3 months, and 17 days. What was his name?

2. Three other men have won a major in the open era before their 18th birthday. How many can you name?

3. Martina Hingis became the youngest winner of a Grand Slam in the open era when she won the 1997 Australian Open, but how old was she?
a. 15 years 189 days   b. 15 years 327 days
c. 16 years 117 days   d. 16 years 214 days

4. Two other women have won majors before their 17th birthday in the open era. Can you name them both?

5. As of September 2024, what is the name of the oldest men's Grand Slam champion in the open era, winning the Australian Open at 37 years, one month and 24 days in 1972?

6. Which player holds the record for the oldest Grand Slam champion in the open era on the women's tour, winning her last major at 35 years, 4 months and 2 days?
a. Martina Navratilova   b. Flavia Pennetta
c. Mary Pierce   d. Serena Williams

7. As of September 2024, Roger Federer holds the record as the oldest winner on the ATP Tour since it was introduced in 1990. How old was he when he won his last title at the 2019 Swiss Indoors?
a. 38 years 2 months   b. 38 years 10 months
c. 39 years 6 months   d. 40 years 1 month

8. Which player became the oldest woman to make her debut as world number one since the rankings began, first capturing the top spot at 28 years and 238 days?

9. A tricky question coming up: what is the name of the player who became the youngest in history to reach the ATP top 10, having done so at just 17 years and 11 days in 1984?

10. Arina Rodinova recently became the oldest player in history to make their debut in the top 100. How old was she when she finally broke this barrier in January 2024?
a. 31 years 122 days   b. 32 years 187 days
c. 33 years 99 days   d. 34 years 52 days

TENNIS THROUGH THE DECADES

PRE 1900

1. In which country did the medieval form of tennis first appear in around the 12th century?
a. France   b. Germany   c. England   d. Argentina

2. The men's singles at Wimbledon was first played in 1877, but when was the ladies singles first played there?
a. 1877   b. 1884   c. 1892   d. 1906

3. Which American male player won the US Open the first seven years it was played from 1881-1887?
a. Malcolm Whitman   b. Laurence Doherty
c. Maurice McLoughlin   d. Richard Sears

4. Which British multi-sport legend won the Wimbledon women's singles five times from 1887-1893?

5. Which British men's player won Wimbledon seven times in the 1880s?
a. William Renshaw   b. John Hartley
c. Spencer Gore   d. Gordon Lowe

6. The women's US Open first started in 1887. When did the first non-American win the title?
a. 1887   b. 1891   c. 1906   d. 1919

7. True or false: the men's French Open was only won by French players from its inception in 1891 to 1900.

8. True or false: medieval tennis game scoring is thought to have gone 15, 30, 45, 60 (game).

9. Which of the following women won all three French Open's that were played in the 19th century?
a. Marguerite Broquedis   b. Julie Vlasto
c. Adine Masson   d. Comtesse de Kermel

10. Which famous 16th-century English monarch was said to be playing tennis when his second wife was beheaded?

1900-1930

1. Which American men's player won seven US Opens from 1901-1911?
a. William Larned   b. Holcombe Ward
c. John Doeg   d. Ellsworth Vines

2. Most of you will have heard of the legendary player Suzanne Lenglen, but how many of the current four majors did she win in her career?
a. 5   b. 8   c. 12   d. 16

3. She won her first major at Wimbledon, but in which year did she achieve this?
a. 1903   b. 1909   c. 1913   d. 1919

4. Suzanne Lenglen had some of the most ridiculous stats in tennis history, such as once only losing five games in the whole tournament on her way to the Wimbledon title, but perhaps her most impressive is her longest win streak. Just how long was this historic winning streak?
a. 98   b. 127   c. 150   d. 181

5. Legendary French tennis player René Lacoste dominated men's tennis in the 1920s before founding the sports fashion company named after him in 1933, which is still sold all over the world today. His nickname was an animal, which later became the logo for his global brand. Which animal is this?
a. Ram   b. Shark   c. Eagle   d. Crocodile

6. How many majors did Lacoste win over his impressive career?
a. 2   b. 4   c. 7   d. 10

7. Which American woman, who would end up winning 19 majors in her career, won her first major at the US Open in 1923?

8. Men's tennis was primarily dominated by French players in the 1920s, with one exception. Which American player won ten majors from 1920-1930, comprising seven US Open and three Wimbledon titles?

9. Which Norwegian-American women's player won eight US Open titles from 1915-1926?

10. Which British men's player won Wimbledon five consecutive times from 1902-1906?
a. Reginald Doherty   b. Algernon Kingscote
c. John Colin Gregory   d. Laurence Doherty

1930-1960

1. Fred Perry was the most dominant force in men's tennis in the 1930s. How many majors did he win in his career?
a. 6   b. 8   c. 10   d. 12

2. This player became the first woman in history to win the Calendar Grand Slam (all four majors in one year) in 1953. What makes this even more incredible is that she was only 18 at the time! She continued to have great success in her teenage years before suffering a tragic career-ending horse riding accident at the age of 19, which forced her to retire. What was her name?

3. How many majors did the player from question 2 win over her short but incredible career?
a. 5   b. 7   c. 9   d. 11

4. Tennis fans all over the world know of the controversial player Bobby Riggs for his highly televised loss against Billie Jean King in a match dubbed 'The Battles of the Sexes', but how many majors did he win while in his prime in the late 1930s and 40s?
a. 0   b. 1   c. 3   d. 6

5. Which of the following women won six Australian Open titles from 1937 to 1951?
a. Joan Hartigan   b. Esna Boyd Robertson
c. Margaret Molesworth   d. Nancye Wynne Bolton

6. Only one of the four majors was held continuously throughout World War II. Which was it?

7. Which nation won the most men's Grand Slams in the 1950s?
a. Australia   b. United Kingdom
c. Sweden   d. United States

8. This Brazilian women's player won the first of her seven singles majors in 1959, making her the most successful South American player in history. What was her name?

9. What is the name of the American men's player who won all six of his career majors consecutively from 1937-1938, making him the first player in history to win the Calendar Grand Slam?

10. Which of the following women won six majors in her career, including three consecutive US Open title from 1948-1950?
a. Margaret Osborne duPont   b. Helen Jacobs
c. Kathleen McKane Godfree   d. Darlene Hard

1960-1980

1. In which year did Argentinian player Guillermo Vilas win the first of his four Grand Slams?
a. 1966   b. 1969   c. 1973   d. 1977

2. Margaret Court is the biggest winner in women's Australian Open history, winning her first title there in 1960. How many times did she win her home tournament?
a. 9   b. 10   c. 11   d. 12

3. True or false: John McEnroe hadn't won any majors by the end of the 1970s.

4. In which year did Billie Jean King win her first major?
a. 1960   b. 1962   c. 1964   d. 1966

5. How many majors did Billie Jean King win before the start of the open era in mid-1968?
a. 1   b. 4   c. 7   d. 11

6. Jimmy Connors dominated tennis in the 1970s and early 80s, but there was one Slam that he never won. Which was it?

7. Roy Emerson won 12 majors from 1961-1967. Where does this place him on the all-time men's Grand Slam winners list?
a. 4th   b. 5th   c. 6th   d. 7th

8. Which British woman won the French Open in 1961 and 1966 before winning her home major at Wimbledon in 1969?

9. Which Spanish men's player won four majors in the 1960s and was ranked by some reporters as the amateur world number one in 1965 and 1966?

10. How many singles majors had Martina Navratilova won before the year 1980?
a. 0   b. 2   c. 5   d. 9

1980-2000

1. Mats Wilander won seven majors over his career, winning two majors three times and one once. Which two majors did he win three times?

2. How many majors did Steffi Graf win before the year 1990?
a. 1   b. 4   c. 8   d. 13

3. Ivan Lendl went on an amazing run of consecutive US Open finals in the 1980s. How many years in a row did he make it to the final two?
a. 5   b. 6   c. 7   d. 8

4. Two Spanish women won majors during the 1990s. Can you name them both?

5. How old was Boris Becker when he won Wimbledon for the first time in 1985?
a. 16   b. 17   c. 18   d. 19

6. Martina Navratilova completely dominated the sport in the 1980s, with her best results coming at Wimbledon. How many times did she win the grasscourt title?
a. 9   b. 10   c. 11   d. 12

7. Boris Becker wasn't the only German to win a major in 1991. Which other German player won a Slam that year?

8. True or false: both Serena and Venus had won a major before the year 2000.

9. Andre Agassi won his first major in 1992, but which Slam was it?

10. True or false: Martina Hingis won all five of her majors in the 1990s.

2000-2010

1. In which year did Sampras win his 14th and final major?
a. 2002 b. 2003 c. 2004 d. 2005

2. How many French women won a major between 2000 and 2009?
a. 0 b. 1 c. 2 d. 3

3. Lleyton Hewitt won his two majors in 2001 and 2002. Which two did he win?

4. At which major did Kim Clijsters win her first Grand Slam in 2005?

5. How many majors had Roger Federer won by the end of 2009?
a. 9 b. 11 c. 13 d. 15

6. How many times did a Williams sister not win Wimbledon from 2000-2009?
a. 1 b. 2 c. 3 d. 4

7. Which major did Juan Martín del Potro win when he won his only Grand Slam in 2009?

8. How many majors had Serena Williams won by the end of 2009?
a. 11 b. 13 c. 15 d. 17

9. Which Chilean men's player won gold at the 2004 Olympic Games?

10. Which major did Anastasia Myskina win in 2004?

2010-2024

1. Stan Wawrinka won three different majors from 2014-2016. Which is the only major he didn't win in his career?

2. Which nationality is two-time Grand Slam champion Victoria Azarenka?

3. Which men's player won his third Monte Carlo Masters title in 2024?
a. Carlos Alcaraz   b. Alexander Zverev
c. Casper Ruud   d. Stefanos Tsitsipas

4. Which women's player won her second career major at Wimbledon in 2024?

5. Which player did Marin Čilić beat to win the 2014 US Open?

6. Which year did Tomáš Berdych beat Roger Federer and Novak Djokovic to reach the Wimbledon final?
a. 2010   b. 2012   c. 2014   d. 2016

7. Ons Jabeur has come so close to winning a major in the last few years but has come up just short. How many major finals has she made as of September 2024?
a. 1   b. 2   c. 3   d. 4

8. Who did Andy Murray beat in the final of Wimbledon 2016 to win his second trophy at the All England Club?

9. Caroline Wozniacki had three different stints as world number one. When did the Dane first get to the top of the women's game?
a. 2008   b. 2010   c. 2012   d. 2014

10. How many times in Djokovic's incredible career has he won three Grand Slams in a calendar year?
a. 3   b. 4   c. 5   d. 6

11. In which year did Karolína Plíšková reach the top of the world rankings?
a. 2014   b. 2015   c. 2016   d. 2017

12. Who beat Andy Murray in five sets in the quarter-finals of Wimbledon 2017, with the world number one suffering from terrible hip pain at the end of the match?
a. Marin Čilić   b. Milos Raonic
c. Fernando Verdasco   d. Sam Querrey

13. How many weeks has Simona Halep spent as world number one in her career so far?
a. 40   b. 64   c. 88   d. 103

14. Which year did Nick Kyrgios make the final of Wimbledon before losing to Djokovic?
a. 2020   b. 2021   c. 2022   d. 2023

15. Petra Kvitova has won Wimbledon twice over her career. Which two years did she achieve this?
a. 2011 & 2014   b. 2010 & 2015
c. 2012 & 2015   d. 2013 & 2016

CONTROVERSIES & SCANDALS

1. Which player was disqualified from the final of Queens in 2012 whilst leading one set to love after kicking a panel in front of a lines judge, which caused his leg to bleed badly?

2. Which player went viral in 2008 after hitting himself in the head with his racket and drawing blood in the third round of the Miami Open?

3. In which year was Serena Williams controversially docked a game for verbal abuse against the umpire in the final of the US Open, ending in a 6-2 6-4 defeat?
a. 2016   b. 2017   c. 2018   d. 2019

4. In which year was John McEnroe disqualified from the Australian Open for verbal abuse towards the umpire, making him the first person to be disqualified from a major for 27 years?
a. 1982   b. 1985   c. 1988   d. 1990

5. In which year did Monica Seles suffer a terrifying on-court stabbing, causing her to miss the next two years of tennis?
a. 1993   b. 1995   c. 1997   d. 1999

6. In which year was Djokovic held in an immigration detention before being deported from Australia because he was not vaccinated against COVID-19?
a. 2019   b. 2020   c. 2021   d. 2022

7. In which year was Maria Sharapova given a two-year doping ban for testing positive for the banned substance meldonium at the Australian Open?
a. 2016   b. 2017   c. 2018   d. 2019

8. Which 17-year-old accidentally hit chair umpire Arnaud Gabas in the eye after smashing a ball aimlessly into the crowd while playing Kyle Edmund at the 2017 Davis Cup?

9. In which year did Boris Becker serve eight months of his two-and-a-half-year prison sentence for hiding assets and loans from the UK court?
a. 2019   b. 2020   c. 2021   d. 2022

10. Which player looked like he was going to be out of tennis for a while in 2009, after being given a one-year ban for testing positive for cocaine, before managing to get the ban overturned after successfully arguing that it was only in his system because he had kissed a girl who had taken that drug in a nightclub?

GUESS THE TOURNAMENT

1. This tournament is the final Masters 1000 event for male players of the year. It has been sponsored by Rolex since 2017 and is played indoors.

2. This is the first WTA 1000 event of the calendar year and is played on outdoor hard courts. Iga Świątek has dominated the tournament in recent years, winning it each year from 2022-2024.

3. This international indoor men's hard court tournament has been held annually since 2017 and is contested between Team World and Team Europe.

4. This international mixed-gender hard court tournament is held in Australia in the build-up to the Australian Open. Six groups consisting of three different countries compete in a round-robin format, with 500 points up for grabs for the eventual winner. It was held for the first time in 2022/23 and was won by Germany.

5. This is the second WTA 1000 event held in China of the year, as well as the final WTA 1000 of the year. It debuted on the WTA in 2014 but was not held from 2020 to 2023 due to COVID-19.

6. This build-up tournament to Wimbledon is held in Central Europe. It was upgraded to an ATP Tour 500 in 2009 and has been won by Roger Federer ten times.

7. This is the final 1000 event for the ATP and WTA Tour before the French Open. It is held in the second week of May every year and was won by Świątek and Zverev in 2024.

8. This build-up tournament to Wimbledon is held on grass courts in the South of England on both the WTA and ATP Tour. It is a WTA 500 event and an ATP 250 event and was won by Daria Kasatkina and Taylor Fritz in 2024.

9. These two 1000 events are held in March. Winning both is referred to as the 'Sunshine Double'.

10. This annual Masters 1000 event is held in October and is the only one on the ATP Tour to be played in Asia.

11. This WTA and ATP 1000 event is the second oldest active tournament in the world behind Wimbledon, first being played in 1881. It was held in August 2024 and won by Jessica Pegula and Alexei Popyrin.

12. This unofficial ATP event debuted in 2017 and features the eight best-ranked players aged 20 and under. It was originally held in Milan, Italy, before being moved to Jeddah, Saudi Arabia, in 2023.

13.   This WTA 500 and ATP 250 event is held annually in January in Australia as part of the build-up to the Australian Open. It was won by Elena Rybakina and Grigor Dimitrov in 2024.

14.   This annual ATP Masters 1000 event is played on clay courts in France in April. It is the third Masters 1000 event of the year on the ATP Tour.

15.   This ATP and WTA 1000 event, founded in 1899, is the final 1000 event held in America of the year. It was won by Jannik Sinner and Aryna Sabalenka in 2024.

RULES

1. True or false: if a player hits a shot around the net post, it is considered an illegal shot and doesn't count.

2. True or false: if a player hits a shot with a lot of backspin that lands on the opponent's side before spinning back and bouncing on their side, it is considered an error, and the point is given to the opponent.

3. True or false: although it can be seen as unsportsmanlike, an underarm serve is always legal in tennis.

4. What is it called when a player's foot either goes over the baseline or crosses the centre mark of the baseline before making contact with their serve?

5. What are the wooden sticks called that prop a doubles net up in the tramlines to make the net the correct height for a game of singles?

6. True or false: a player is never allowed to touch the net during a point.

7. True or false: a player is never allowed to reach over and hit the opponent's ball while it is on their side of the court.

45

8. True or false: a shot is considered legal if a player accidentally hits it twice, also known as a double-hit, but it was performed in one single continuous movement.

9. True or false: if a player completely misses the ball with their racket on a serve, it is not considered a fault, and they can replay that serve without penalty.

10. True or false: it is considered an illegal shot if a player throws their racket to hit an out-of-reach ball, which then miraculously hits the ball over the net while it is not in contact with their hand.

DOUBLES

1. The Bryan brothers are arguably the greatest men's doubles pair ever to play tennis, but one brother has won two more majors than the other. Which brother has won the most?

2. How many majors has this brother won?
a. 18   b. 20   c. 22   d. 24

3. One player stands out by far as the greatest women's doubles player in history, winning ten more Grand Slams than second place. What is her name?

4. How many women's doubles majors did she win over her incredible career?
a. 24   b. 28   c. 31   d. 35

5. Amazingly, Jamie Murray beat his younger brother to the first Wimbledon title, winning the mixed doubles in 2007. Who was his partner?
a. Daniela Hantuchova   b. Ana Ivanovic
c. Venus Williams   d. Jelena Jankovic

6. Billie Jean King has been the greatest women's doubles player in the last 100 years at Wimbledon. How many times did she win the women's doubles at the All England Club?
a. 9   b. 10   c. 11   d. 12

7. Which player became the oldest first-time world number won when he won his first major at the 2024 Australian Open at the age of 43 with his partner Matthew Ebden?

8. Serena and Venus are not only some of the most successful singles players in history but also doubles. How many women's doubles majors did they win?
a. 8   b. 10   c. 12   d. 14

9. One player stands out as the best men's doubles player at Wimbledon of all time, with nine wins at the All England Club. What is his name?

10. How many combined women's doubles and mixed doubles majors did Margaret Court win over her career?
a. 28   b. 32   c. 36   d. 40

11. Which Indian men's doubles player won ten mixed doubles Grand Slams from 1999-2016, making him the most successful men's mixed doubles player in the last 50 years?

12. Which British doubles player partnered Harri Heliövaara to win the men's doubles at Wimbledon in 2024?

13. Which major did Coco Gauff and Kateřina Siniaková win together in 2024, making it the first doubles major for Coco in her career?

14. Which fellow Czech player did Kateřina Siniaková partner in from 2018-2023 to win seven women's doubles majors, making them the most successful pairing in women's doubles in recent history?

15. Which year did Thanasi Kokkinakis and Nick Kyrgios win the men's doubles at the Australian Open?
a. 2016 b. 2018 c. 2020 d. 2022

16. This American doubles player won 21 women's doubles majors from 1981-1991, including the calendar doubles Grand Slam in 1984. What is her name?

17. Two Australian players won 16 and 17 men's doubles majors in the 1960s and 1970s. Can you name them both?

18. Martina Hingis won nine women's doubles majors from 1996-2002 before making a comeback many years later and winning four more. When did she win her final women's doubles Grand Slam?
a. 2015 b. 2017 c. 2019 d. 2021

19. How many men's doubles majors have Rajeev Ram and Joe Salisbury won together as of September 2024?
a. 1 b. 2 c. 4 d. 7

20. Which Indian player won three women's doubles majors from 2015 to 2016?

TENNIS BY COUNTRY

1. How many different Spanish men's players have won a major in the 21st century?
a. 4   b. 5   c. 6   d. 7

2. How many different American women have won a major in the 21st century?
a. 6   b. 7   c. 8   d. 9

3. Which nation has won more men's majors in the open era: Serbia or Australia?

4. How many British women have won a major in the open era?
a. 2   b. 3   c. 4   d. 5

5. How many men's majors were won by South American players in the 21st century?
a. 2   b. 4   c. 6   d. 8

6. The countries and order of the top three all-time Grand Slam-winning nations is the same for both men and women since the start of tennis. Can you guess what three countries these are and place them in the correct order?

7. Which nation has won more men's majors since the open era: Sweden or Spain?

8. How many Asian women have won a Grand Slam in the 21st century?
a. 1 b. 2 c. 3 d. 4

9. How many men's majors have been won by players from Asia since the start of the open era?
a. 0 b. 1 c. 3 d. 6

10. How many majors have Serbian women won in the 21st century?
a. 1 b. 2 c. 3 d. 4

11. Which is the only Grand Slam that has not been won by an American men's player in the 21st century?

12. How many French women have won a major since the start of the open era?
a. 2 b. 4 c. 6 d. 8

13. Who was the last men's Czech player to have won a Grand Slam?

14. Who was the last Spanish woman before Garbiñe Muguruza to have won a Grand Slam, doing so in 1998?

15. Who is the last men's player from Sweden to have won a major?

OLYMPICS

1. Who won the women's singles title at the 2024 Olympics?

2. Which Caribbean island does 2016 Olympics champion Monica Puig come from?
a. Puerto Rico   b. Cuba   c. Hispaniola   d. Jamaica

3. Who did Murray destroy in three sets to win gold at the 2012 Olympics?
a. Rafa Nadal   b. Novak Djokovic
c. David Ferrer   d. Roger Federer

4. In which year did Venus Williams win singles gold at the Olympics?
a. 2000   b. 2004   c. 2008   d. 2012

5. The 1996 Olympics was dominated by American players, with the US winning gold in both the men's and women's singles. Which two players won this year?
a. Pete Sampras and Jennifer Capriati
b. Andre Agassi and Martina Navratilova
c. Jim Courier and Serena Williams
d. Andre Agassi and Lindsay Davenport

6. Which European player won singles gold at the 2004 Olympics?
a. Justine Henin   b. Maria Sharapova
c. Kim Clijsters   d. Amélie Mauresmo

7. Which men's player won gold at the 2020 Olympics after crushing Karen Khachanov 6-3 6-1 in the final?

8. Who did Novak Djokovic beat in the final of the 2024 Olympic Games to win the final trophy that was missing from his career?

9. Which men's doubles pair won gold at the 2024 Olympics?
a. Austin Krajicek and Rajeev Ram
b. Taylor Fritz and Tommy Paul
c. Marin Čilić and Ivan Dodig
d. Matthew Ebden and John Peers

10. Which surprise player from Switzerland won gold in the women's singles at the 2020 Olympics?

11. Tennis stopped being part of the Olympics for 64 years during the 20th century. When was it first reintroduced?
a. 1976 b. 1980 c. 1984 d. 1988

12. Who won the women's singles gold the first year it was reintroduced?

13. Which Italian men's player won bronze at the 2024 Olympics?

14. Which Russian woman won gold at the 2008 Olympic Games?

15. Which player from Chile did Rafael Nadal beat in the final of the 2008 Olympic Games?

16. Which Russian men's player won gold at the 2000 Olympic Games?

17. Which player from Germany did Monica Puig beat in the final of the 2016 Olympics?
a. Julia Goerges   b. Angelique Kerber
c. Sabine Lisicki   d. Annika Beck

18. How many sets did Murray need to beat Del Potro and win his second Olympic gold medal in 2016?
a. Three   b. Four   c. Five

19. Who did Sara Errani partner to win doubles gold at the 2024 Olympics?

20. Which woman from Croatia won silver in the singles at the 2024 Olympics?

MATCH THE NAME

Here are 13 jumbled-up first and surnames of players currently competing on the ATP Tour. How many can you match up?

David	Tabilo
Borna	Marozsán
Alejandro	Monteiro
Roman	Popyrin
Ben	Humbert
Fábián	Goffin
Holger	Sonego
Thiago	Shelton
Ugo	Cerúndolo
Lorenzo	Ćorić
Alexei	Ruud
Francisco	Rune
Casper	Safiullin

Here are 13 jumbled-up first and surnames of players currently competing on the WTA Tour. How many can you match up?

Maria	Yastremska
Yulia	Cîrstea
Dayana	Kostyuk
Jasmine	Andreeva
Taylor	Putintseva
Sorana	Kasatkina
Mirra	Samsonova
Katie	Mertens
Liudmila	Townsend
Daria	Jabeur
Marta	Sakkari
Elise	Boulter
Ons	Paolini

MATCH THE NATIONALITY

Here are 13 jumbled-up players currently competing on the ATP Tour and their nationalities. How many can you match up?

Players	Nationalities
Grigor Dimitrov	Australian
Sebastián Báez	Finnish
Nicolás Jarry	Czech
Jordan Thompson	British
Matteo Arnaldi	Argentine
Jiří Lehečka	Serbian
Jan-Lennard Struff	Bulgarian
Tallon Griekspoor	Japanese
Cameron Norrie	Greek
Yoshihito Nishioka	Italian
Dušan Lajović	German
Emil Ruusuvuori	Dutch
Stefanos Tsitsipas	Chilean

Here are 13 jumbled-up players currently competing on the WTA Tour and their nationalities. How many can you match up?

Players	Nationalities
Elena Rybakina	French
Jeļena Ostapenko	American
Lulu Sun	Ukrainian
Anhelina Kalinina	Swiss
Madison Keys	Kazakhstani
Yuan Yue	Czech
Caroline Garcia	New Zealander
Leylah Fernandez	Brazilian
Magda Linette	Belarusian
Barbora Krejčíková	Polish
Beatriz Haddad Maia	Canadian
Aryna Sabalenka	Latvian
Viktorija Golubic	Chinese

ATP BY NUMBERS

ATP by Numbers is 10 rounds of men's tennis questions, starting with 10 answers and counting down to 1. How many can you get right?

10 players who have won the most majors in the open era	9 nations with the most major wins in the open era	Last 8 separate players to have won the French Open

Last 7 separate players to win the ATP Finals	Last 6 American players to be ranked world number one	5 different Wimbledon winners of the 1990s (1990 at the top)

Last 4 South American players to win a major	Last 3 players to win Queens	Last 2 players from a country starting with A to win the US Open

1 French player to win a major in the open era

WTA BY NUMBERS

WTA by Numbers is 10 rounds of women's tennis questions, starting with 10 answers and counting down to 1. How many can you get right?

10 players who have spent the most time as world number one	Last 9 separate Wimbledon singles champions	Last 8 Americans to win a major
		*Monica Seles is not being counted as an American player here

62

Last 7 separate French Open singles champions	Last 6 separate world number ones	Last 5 players to win multiple Grand Slams in a season
		*Including the 2024 US Open

Last 4 separate WTA Finals champions	Last 3 separate Australians to win a major	The two majors won by Garbiñe Muguruza

Last player to beat Serena Williams in a major final

ANSWERS

GUESS THE PLAYER

1. Gaël Monfils
2. Sara Errani
3. Nikolay Davydenko
4. Lindsay Davenport
5. Matteo Berrettini
6. Sofia Kenin
7. Gilles Simon
8. Jelena Janković
9. Dan Evans
10. Svetlana Kuznetsova
11. Ernests Gulbis
12. Bianca Andreescu
13. Jürgen Melzer
14. Sabine Lisicki
15. Carlos Moyá
16. Sloane Stephens
17. Gastón Gaudio
18. Danielle Collins
19. Ričardas Berankis
20. Jana Novotná
21. Dustin Brown
22. Beatriz Haddad Maia
23. Sebastian Korda
24. Elena Dementieva
25. Arthur Fils
26. Leylah Fernandez
27. Adrian Mannarino
28. Paula Badosa
29. Sumit Nagal
30. Harriet Dart

RECORDS

1. d - Feliciano López
2. c - 74
3. d - Jimmy Connors
4. b - Chris Evert
5. c - 7
6. a - Martina Navratilova
7. d - Sam Groth
8. d - Miami
9. c - Andre Agassi
10. d - 24
11. Rod Laver
12. b - 21
13. Milos Raonic
14. a & e - Chris Evert and Martina Navratilova
15. Pete Sampras
16. d & e - Germany and Australia
17. c - 4th
18. a - Steffi Graf
19. Olivier Rochus
20. b - Lindsay Davenport
21. Andre Agassi and Lleyton Hewitt
22. b - 4 hours 44 minutes
23. John Isner and Nicolas Mahut
24. c - 70-68
25. d - 377

GRAND SLAMS

1. d - 1976
2. b - 2000
3. Garbiñe Muguruza
4. a - Arthur Ashe
5. Martina Hingis
6. c - 7
7. Andy Murray, Stan Wawrinka and Marin Čilić
8. b - 2018
9. c - 3
10. a - 1936
11. Australian Open and French Open
12. d - 14
13. a - 2008
14. Albert Costa
15. c - £2.7 million ($3.6 million)
16. Wimbledon (1877), US Open (1881), Australian Open (1905), French Open (1925)
17. Sam Stosur
18. Gustavo Kuerten, Lleyton Hewitt, Gastón Gaudio and Juan Martín del Potro
19. Europe
20. Andrés Gómez
21. c - 8
22. a - 2003
23. c - 3
24. b - Jo-Wilfried Tsonga

25. Hana Mandlíková
26. b - 2012
27. US Open
28. Francesca Schiavone and Flavia Pennetta
29. c - 17
30. Thomas Johansson in 2002
31. French Open
32. Patrick Rafter
33. a - 11
34. d - 2001
35. c - 2
36. b - 4
37. Jeļena Ostapenko
38. d - 7
39. d - 2006
40. b - 2005
41. c - 7
42. Ilie Năstase
43. a - 6
44. a - 5
45. d - 2001 & 2002

TERMINOLOGY

1. Winning 6-0, 6-0
2. d - Shank
3. a & d - Tweener and hotdog
4. d - Kick serve
5. Hawk-eye
6. d - Half volley
7. a - Mini break
8. c & e - Super tiebreak and match tiebreak
9. a - T serve
10. c - Flat

OLDEST & YOUNGEST

1. Michael Chang
2. Boris Becker, Mats Wilander and Björn Borg
3. c - 16 years 117 days
4. Monica Seles and Tracy Austin
5. Ken Rosewall
6. d - Serena Williams
7. a - 38 years 2 months
8. Angelique Kerber
9. Aaron Krickstein
10. d - 34 years 52 days

TENNIS THROUGH THE DECADES

PRE 1900

1. a - France
2. b - 1884
3. d - Richard Sears
4. Lottie Dod
5. a - William Renshaw
6. b - 1891
7. False - The first-ever winner was British player H. Briggs. After this, no foreigner won it until 1933
8. True, 45 was changed to 40 at some point in about the 16th century
9. c - Adine Masson
10. Henry VIII

1900-1930

1. a - William Larned
2. b - 8
3. d - 1919
4. d - 181
5. d - Crocodile
6. c - 7

7. Helen Wills Moody
8. Bill Tilden
9. Molla Mallory
10. d - Laurence Doherty

1930-1960

1. b - 8
2. Maureen Connolly
3. c - 9
4. c - 3
5. d - Nancye Wynne Bolton
6. US Open
7. a - Australia
8. Maria Bueno
9. Don Budge
10. a - Margaret Osborne duPont

1960-1980

1. d - 1977
2. c - 11
3. False - He won his first in 1979
4. d - 1966
5. b - 4
6. French Open
7. b - 5th
8. Ann Haydon Jones

9. Manuel Santana
10. b - 2

1980-2000

1. Australian Open and French Open
2. c - 8
3. d - 8
4. Arantxa Sánchez Vicario and Conchita Martínez
5. b - 17
6. a - 9
7. Michael Stich
8. False - Serena won her first in 1999, but Venus didn't win her first until 2000
9. Wimbledon
10. True

2000-2010

1. a - 2002
2. c - 2
3. US Open and Wimbledon
4. US Open
5. d - 15
6. b - 2
7. US Open
8. a - 11
9. Nicolás Massú
10. French Open

2010-2024

1. Wimbledon
2. Belarusian
3. d - Stefanos Tsitsipas
4. Barbora Krejčíková
5. Kei Nishikori
6. a - 2010
7. c - 3
8. Milos Raonic
9. b - 2010
10. b - 4
11. d - 2017
12. d - Sam Querrey
13. b - 64
14. c - 2022
15. a - 2011 & 2014

CONTROVERSIES & SCANDALS

1. David Nalbandian
2. Mikhail Youzhny
3. c - 2018
4. d - 1990
5. a - 1993
6. d - 2022
7. a - 2016
8. Denis Shapovalov
9. d - 2022
10. Richard Gasquet

GUESS THE TOURNAMENT

1. Paris Masters
2. Qatar Open
3. Laver Cup
4. United Cup
5. Wuhan Open
6. Swiss Indoors (Basel)
7. Italian Open (Rome)
8. Eastbourne International
9. Indian Wells Open and Miami Open
10. Shanghai Masters
11. Canadian Open
12. Next Generation ATP Finals
13. Brisbane International
14. Monte-Carlo Masters
15. Cincinnati Open

RULES

1. False
2. False
3. True
4. Foot fault
5. Singles sticks
6. True
7. False - if a ball has bounced on your side before spinning back over to their side, a player is allowed to reach over and play the ball
8. True
9. False
10. True (check out Bublik's amazing shot, match point down, against Shelton in August 2024)

DOUBLES

1. Mike Bryan
2. a - 18
3. Martina Navratilova
4. c - 31
5. d - Jelena Jankovic
6. b - 10
7. Rohan Bopanna
8. d - 14
9. Todd Woodbridge
10. d - 40
11. Leander Paes
12. Henry Patten
13. French Open
14. Barbora Krejčíková
15. d - 2022
16. Pam Shriver
17. Roy Emerson and John Newcombe
18. b - 2017
19. c - 4
20. Sania Mirza

TENNIS BY COUNTRY

1. a - 4
2. b - 7
3. Serbia - and it is all thanks to Novak Djokovic
4. c - 4
5. b - 4
6. United States, Australia, Great Britain
7. Spain
8. c - 3
9. a - 0
10. a - 1
11. French Open
12. a - 2
13. Petr Korda
14. Arantxa Sánchez Vicario
15. Thomas Johansson

OLYMPICS

1. Zheng Qinwen
2. a - Puerto Rico
3. d - Roger Federer
4. a - 2000
5. d - Andre Agassi and Lindsay Davenport
6. a - Justine Henin
7. Alexander Zverev
8. Carlos Alcaraz
9. d - Matthew Ebden and John Peers
10. Belinda Bencic
11. d - 1988
12. Steffi Graf
13. Lorenzo Musetti
14. Elena Dementieva
15. Fernando González
16. Yevgeny Kafelnikov
17. b - Angelique Kerber
18. b - Four
19. Jasmine Paolini
20. Donna Vekić

MATCH THE NAME

ATP

David Goffin
Borna Ćorić
Alejandro Tabilo
Roman Safiullin
Ben Shelton
Fábián Marozsán
Holger Rune

Thiago Monteiro
Ugo Humbert
Lorenzo Sonego
Alexei Popyrin
Francisco Cerúndolo
Casper Ruud

WTA

Maria Sakkari
Yulia Putintseva
Dayana Yastremska
Jasmine Paolini
Taylor Townsend
Sorana Cîrstea
Mirra Andreeva

Katie Boulter
Liudmila Samsonova
Daria Kasatkina
Marta Kostyuk
Elise Mertens
Ons Jabeur

MATCH THE NATIONALITY

ATP

Grigor Dimitrov - Bulgarian

Sebastián Báez - Argentine

Nicolás Jarry - Chilean

Jordan Thompson - Australian

Matteo Arnaldi - Italian

Jiří Lehečka - Czech

Jan-Lennard Struff - German

Tallon Griekspoor - Dutch

Cameron Norrie - British

Yoshihito Nishioka - Japanese

Dušan Lajović - Serbian

Emil Ruusuvuori - Finnish

Stefanos Tsitsipas - Greek

WTA

Elena Rybakina - Kazakhstani

Jeļena Ostapenko - Latvian

Lulu Sun - New Zealander

Anhelina Kalinina - Ukrainian

Madison Keys - American

Yuan Yue - Chinese

Caroline Garcia - French

Leylah Fernandez - Canadian

Magda Linette - Polish

Barbora Krejčíková - Czech

Beatriz Haddad Maia - Brazilian

Aryna Sabalenka - Belarusian

Viktorija Golubic - Swiss

ATP BY NUMBERS

10 players who have won the most majors in the open era	9 nations with the most major wins in the open era	Last 8 separate players to have won the French Open
Novak Djokovic	United States	Carlos Alcaraz
Rafael Nadal	Spain	Novak Djokovic
Roger Federer	Sweden	Rafael Nadal
Pete Sampras	Serbia	Stan Wawrinka
Björn Borg	Switzerland	Roger Federer
Jimmy Connors	Australia	Gastón Gaudio
Ivan Lendl	Czech Republic	Juan Carlos Ferrero
Andre Agassi	Germany	Albert Costa
John McEnroe	Argentina	
Mats Wilander		

Last 7 separate players to win the ATP Finals	Last 6 American players to be ranked world number one	5 different Wimbledon winners of the 1990s (1990 at the top)
Novak Djokovic	Andy Roddick	Stefan Edberg
Alexander Zverev	Andre Agassi	Michael Stich
Daniil Medvedev	Pete Sampras	Andre Agassi
Stefanos Tsitsipas	Jim Courier	Pete Sampras
Grigor Dimitrov	John McEnroe	Richard Krajicek
Andy Murray	Jimmy Connors	
Roger Federer		

Last 4 South American players to win a major	Last 3 players to win Queens	Last 2 players from a country starting with A to win the US Open
Juan Martín del Potro	Tommy Paul	Dominic Thiem
Gastón Gaudio	Carlos Alcaraz	Juan Martín del Potro
Gustavo Kuerten	Matteo Berrettini	
Andrés Gómez		

1 French player to win a major in the open era
Yannick Noah

WTA BY NUMBERS

10 players who have spent the most time as world number one	Last 9 separate Wimbledon singles champions	Last 8 Americans to win a major
Steffi Graf	Barbora Krejčíková	Coco Gauff
Martina Navratilova	Markéta Vondroušová	Sofia Kenin
Serena Williams	Elena Rybakina	Sloane Stephens
Chris Evert	Ashleigh Barty	Serena Williams
Martina Hingis	Simona Halep	Venus Williams
Monica Seles	Angelique Kerber	Jennifer Capriati
Ashleigh Barty	Garbiñe Muguruza	Lindsay Davenport
Iga Świątek	Serena Williams	Martina Navratilova
Justine Henin	Petra Kvitová	
Lindsay Davenport		

Last 7 separate French Open singles champions	Last 6 separate world number ones	Last 5 players to win multiple Grand Slams in a season
Iga Świątek	Iga Świątek	Aryna Sabalenka
Barbora Krejčíková	Aryna Sabalenka	Iga Świątek
Ashleigh Barty	Ashleigh Barty	Angelique Kerber
Simona Halep	Naomi Osaka	Serena Williams
Jeļena Ostapenko	Simona Halep	Justine Henin
Garbiñe Muguruza	Caroline Wozniacki	
Serena Williams		

Last 4 separate WTA Finals champions	Last 3 separate Australians to win majors	The two majors won by Garbiñe Muguruza
Iga Świątek	Ashleigh Barty	French Open
Caroline Garcia	Samantha Stosur	Wimbledon
Garbiñe Muguruza	Evonne Goolagong Cawley	
Ashleigh Barty		

Last player to beat Serena Williams in a major final
Bianca Andreescu

Printed in Great Britain
by Amazon